SUPER BOWL

SUPER TEAMS

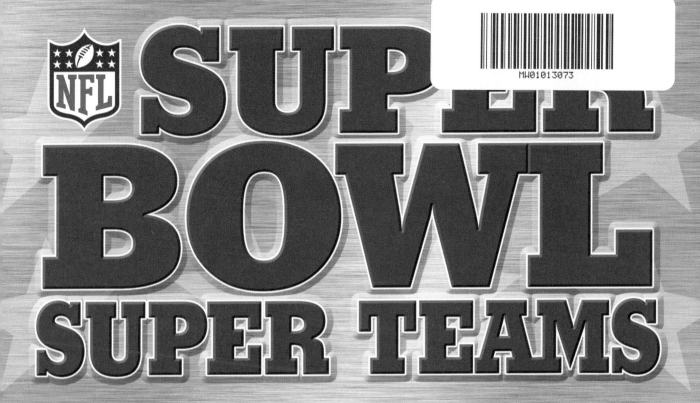

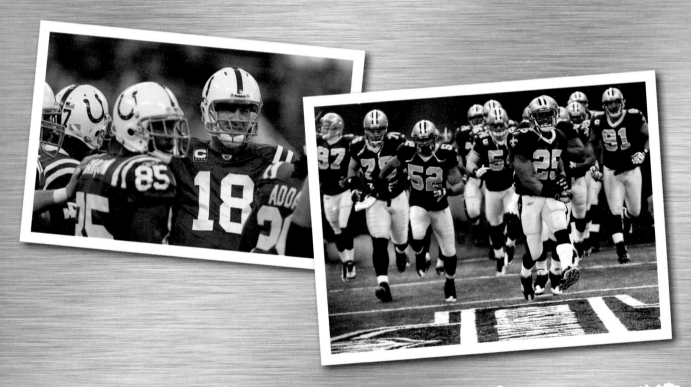

BY JIM GIGLIOTTI

SCHOLASTIC INC.

New York   Toronto   London   Auckland
Sydney   Mexico City   New Delhi   Hong Kong

Contents

Meet the Super Bowl XLIV Champions!

It would be tough to find many football experts who saw this one coming: The New Orleans Saints of the National Football Conference (NFC) beat the Indianapolis Colts of the American Football Conference (AFC) 31–17 to win Super Bowl XLIV in South Florida on February 7, 2010. Quarterback Drew Brees was named the game's Most Valuable Player after passing for 288 yards and two touchdowns to lead the Saints to the first championship in their 43-year history.

COMEBACK KIDS

The Saints equaled the biggest comeback in Super Bowl history in game XLIV. After falling behind 10–0 in the first quarter, it looked as if New Orleans was on the verge of getting clobbered. But the Saints marched from their 11-yard line to the Colts' 29-yard line to kick a field goal, then kept Indianapolis from making a first down the rest of the first half. The only other team to erase a 10-point deficit in the Super Bowl was Washington. The Redskins beat the Denver Broncos 42–10 in Super Bowl XXII after falling behind 10–0 in the first quarter.

SURPRISE!

The biggest play of the Saints' win over the Colts in Super Bowl XLIV was an onside kick to open the second half. It was a bold move. Onside kicks almost never work when they are a desperation move by a team trailing near the end of a game. But in this case, the Colts were taken totally by surprise. The Saints recovered, and drove to a go-ahead touchdown.

BIG PLAY II

The second big play for the Saints was the one that sealed the outcome. After the Saints went ahead 24–17 in the fourth quarter on Drew Brees' 2-yard touchdown pass to tight end Jeremy Shockey and a two-point conversion, the Colts began marching toward a potential tying touchdown. But cornerback Tracy Porter, a native of Port Allen, Louisiana, intercepted a pass and returned it 74 yards for a touchdown. After that, it was all over but the celebrating!

Who's Next?

Who will win the Super Bowl in the 2010 season? In today's NFL, don't count anybody out! After all, before 2009, the Saints hadn't been to the playoffs since 2006. In fact, they'd only been to the postseason six times in their 42-season history, and they had never made it to the Super Bowl. Here are a few teams that could win Super Bowl XLV:

THE SAINTS

The Saints' offense was very powerful in 2009, and their defense has a lot of good, young players. Plus, it's been done before: Eight teams have successfully defended their Super Bowl win with another championship. But it seems to be getting harder. Three of the four Super Bowl champs before the Saints didn't even make the playoffs the following season, let alone make it back to the Big Game.

TEAMS THAT CAME CLOSE

The Colts have been in the Super Bowl chase just about every year in the 2000s. (They've made the playoffs every year since 2002.) The New York Jets were the surprise team of pro football in 2009 and played the Colts tough in the AFC Championship Game. The Minnesota Vikings had a chance to beat the Saints in the NFC Championship Game before losing in overtime. Will 40-year-old Brett Favre be back to quarterback the Vikings in 2010? We may not know until close to the start of the season!

THE HOMETOWN FACTOR

No NFL team ever has won the Super Bowl in its home stadium. This season's Super Bowl will be played at Cowboys Stadium in North Texas. The Cowboys would love to make it to the Super Bowl in their backyard!

EVERYBODY ELSE

Okay, that's cheating. But since hardly anybody saw the Saints coming, maybe it's time for some other unexpected team to take the next step. Perhaps it's time for the San Diego Chargers or Philadelphia Eagles to win their first Super Bowl. Or maybe a young team such as the Atlanta Falcons or Houston Texans, both of which just missed out on the playoffs in 2009. Or maybe the Pittsburgh Steelers or Green Bay Packers will return to the top. Or maybe . . . well, what team is your pick?

Super Bowl Dynasties:
BRADY'S BUNCH

Football is the ultimate team sport. It takes all 11 players on offense to make a play work. If one player doesn't do his job, whether he's blocking, catching, throwing, or running—well, a play just won't work very well.

Still, there's no position more important than quarterback. Every Super Bowl champion has had a great player running the show. The New England Patriots had one of the best when they played the St. Louis Rams in Super Bowl XXXVI in the 2001 season. It's just that no one knew it yet! Tom Brady was a young quarterback who took over when veteran Drew Bledsoe was hurt early in the season. No one gave the Patriots much of a chance against the mighty Rams. But late in the game, Brady marched his team to a field goal as time ran out. Patriots 20, Rams 17!

THREE OUT OF FOUR

Quarterback Tom Brady and the Patriots were just getting warmed up when they upset the Rams in Super Bowl XXXVI. While their quarterback eventually became a nationally known superstar, the Patriots of the early 2000s were mostly a team that didn't have a lot of star players. Instead, they were so good because they all worked together well. They also went on to win Super Bowl XXXVIII in the 2003 season and Super Bowl XXXIX in the 2004 season. They were only the second team to win three Super Bowls in a stretch of four seasons.

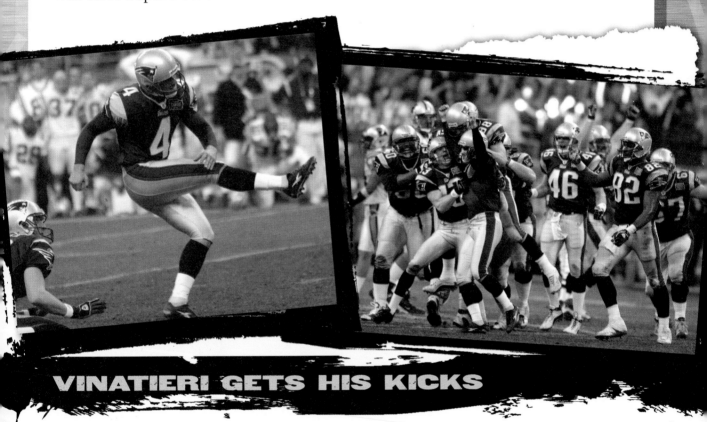

VINATIERI GETS HIS KICKS

Ever imagine kicking the game-winning field goal for your team in the Super Bowl? The ball goes through the uprights, the clock ticks down to 0:00, and you're carried off the field by your teammates as confetti streams down onto the field!

Only one player ever fulfilled that dream. Adam Vinatieri kicked the game-winning field goal as time ran out in the Patriots' 20–17 win over the Rams in Super Bowl XXXVI. What's more, Vinatieri's field goals also made the difference in New England's 32–29 win over the Carolina Panthers in Super Bowl XXXVIII (that kick came with four seconds left) and its 24–21 win over the Philadelphia Eagles in Super Bowl XXXIX (that kick came midway through the fourth quarter).

More Champions of the 2000s

The New England Patriots won three Super Bowls in the 2000s, but the one that got away still hurts. New England won all 16 of its regular-season games in 2007, then two more games in the playoffs. But the New York Giants ended New England's bid for perfection with a 17–14 upset in Super Bowl XLII.

It was especially hard for Patriots' fans because the team came this close to being perfect. New England was ahead 14–10 in the fourth quarter when the Giants got the ball back for the last time. One of quarterback Eli Manning's passes was almost intercepted. On another play, Manning looked like he would be sacked for sure. Somehow, he escaped to throw a pass downfield that was caught by receiver David Tyree on the top of his helmet! The winning pass came with only 35 seconds left.

SIX FOR THE STEELERS

The Pittsburgh Steelers won four Super Bowls in the 1970s, and their players talked about winning "one for the thumb." (Meaning a fifth Super Bowl ring to fill one hand.) It took a while, but the Steelers finally got their next Super Bowl win in the 2005 season. That year, they beat the Seattle Seahawks 21–10 in Super Bowl XL. Fortunately for Steelers' fans, they didn't have to wait as long for another title. It came in the 2008 season. Pittsburgh beat Arizona in one of the most exciting Super Bowls ever, 27–23.

THE COLTS' TURN

No team has been as consistent in the 2000s as the Indianapolis Colts. They made the playoffs all but one time in the 10 seasons of the decade. Once they got to the playoffs, though, it usually was a different story. The Colts always were good—just not quite good enough. Finally, in the 2006 season, quarterback Peyton Manning took his team to the Super Bowl. And this time, the Colts were plenty good enough. They beat the Chicago Bears 29–17 in Super Bowl XLI.

Super Bowl Dynasties:
HOW 'BOUT THEM COWBOYS?!

In one of their most important games of the 1990s, the Dallas Cowboys beat the San Francisco 49ers in an NFC Championship Game to reach the Super Bowl. Head coach Jimmy Johnson was so excited that in the locker room after the game, he whooped, "How 'bout them Cowboys?!" That became the rallying cry for Dallas and its fans during the decade, when the Cowboys were the NFL's best team.

Dallas has been pretty good for most of its history. The Cowboys had one of the best teams of the 1970s and one of the best teams in the 1980s, but there always seemed to be one team just a little better, like the Steelers or the 49ers. Then the Cowboys hit a rough spot in the late 1980s. They won only one game in 1989. By 1991, though, Johnson had the team back in the playoffs. In 1992, Dallas was on top. The Cowboys knocked off the rival 49ers in the NFC title game, then routed Buffalo 52-17 in Super Bowl XXVII in one of the most lopsided championship games ever.

The Cowboys beat the Bills again in Super Bowl XXVIII the next season (this time it was a little closer), then beat the Steelers in game XXX in the 1995 season. They were the first team to win the Super Bowl three times in a four-season span.

THE TRIPLETS

What do you call three superstars on the same Super Bowl-winning team's offense? The "Triplets"! That was the collective nickname of Cowboys quarterback Troy Aikman, running back Emmitt Smith, and wide receiver Michael Irvin. Together, they made Dallas' offense go in the 1990s. All three are members of the Pro Football Hall of Fame.

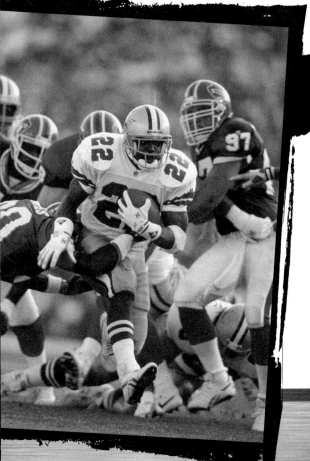

ECSTASY AND AGONY

It was great to be a Buffalo Bills' fan in the 1990s—and not so great at the same time! With quarterback Jim Kelly running the no-huddle offense, the Bills played an exciting, wide-open style of football that produced a lot of points, and a lot of wins. The Bills did something no other team has done. Beginning in 1990, they played in the Super Bowl four times in a row. That's the good news. The bad news: They lost all four games.

More Champions of the 1990s

Lots of football players talk about going out on top. Denver Broncos star quarterback John Elway really did it.

The Broncos came close to winning it all several times in the 1980s, but Elway couldn't do it all himself. So the Broncos got him some help in running back Terrell Davis. With Davis running wild, the Broncos beat the Green Bay Packers 31–24 in Super Bowl XXXII in the 1997 season. The next year, Denver beat the Atlanta Falcons 34–19 in game XXXIII.

Elway didn't have to do much in the Broncos' first Super Bowl win because Davis scored three touchdowns. Against the Falcons, though, Elway passed for 336 yards and ran for a touchdown. He was named the game's Most Valuable Player—and then he retired. He is the only player ever to be the Super Bowl MVP in the last game of his career.

YOUNG STRIKES GOLD

Quarterback Joe Montana helped the San Francisco 49ers win four Super Bowls in the 1980s, but the team traded him to Kansas City in 1992. His successor at quarterback, Steve Young, had some big shoes to fill. In 1994, Young led the 49ers to a 49–26 victory over the San Diego Chargers in Super Bowl XXIX by passing for a record six touchdowns. It was San Francisco's fifth Super Bowl win in 14 seasons. After that, the team's dynasty quietly faded away. Though the 49ers have recently showed signs of getting better again, they haven't been to the playoffs since 2002.

THE GREATEST SHOW ON TURF

The Rams of the late 1990s built perhaps the greatest offense in NFL history. With quarterback Kurt Warner, running back Marshall Faulk, and receivers Isaac Bruce and Torry Holt, they were called the "Greatest Show on Turf." It was a defensive play, though, that saved the Rams' 23–16 victory over the Tennessee Titans in Super Bowl XXXIV. Late in the game, the Titans drove to the Rams' 10-yard line with time for one more play. Kevin Dyson caught a short pass over the middle and headed to the goal line. But linebacker Mike Jones wrapped him up and tackled him. Dyson reached for the goal line—one yard short! The Rams won.

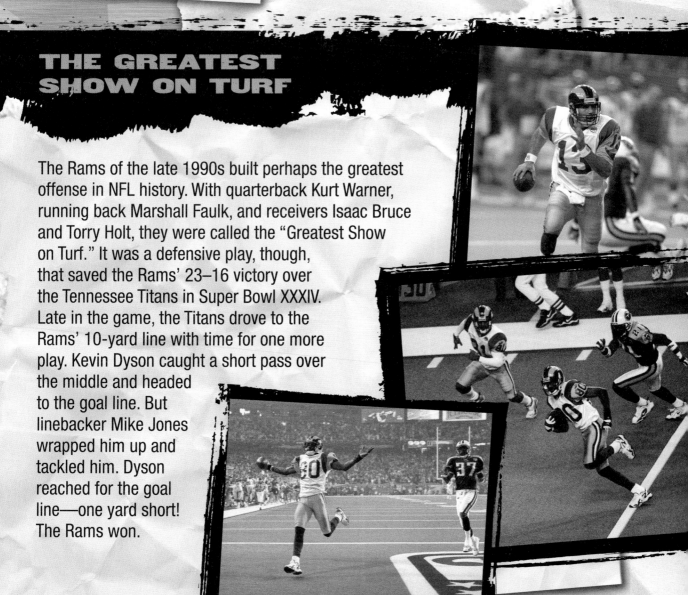

Super Bowl Dynasties:
JOE KNOWS SUPER BOWLS

Lots of great quarterbacks played in the 1980s: Dan Marino, John Elway, and Jim Kelly were just a few. But the greatest may have been Joe Montana. After all, a quarterback's biggest job is to help his team win championships—and nobody did that better than Montana.

With Montana leading the way, the San Francisco 49ers were the Team of the Eighties, winning four Super Bowls in the decade. Head coach Bill Walsh's West Coast Offense revolutionized football, while Montana's cool under fire was legendary. The West Coast Offense uses short, safe passes, and timing routes between a

16

quarterback and receivers. Walsh didn't invent the West Coast Offense, but he made it popular because it worked so well in San Francisco. Almost every NFL team uses some version of the West Coast Offense now.

In Walsh's final game, Montana led the 49ers on an epic drive to win Super Bowl XXIII against Cincinnati. San Francisco won 20–16 when Montana threw a 10-yard touchdown pass to John Taylor with 34 seconds left.

The next year, the 49ers didn't need any last-minute heroics. Under new coach George Seifert, they won the biggest Super Bowl blowout ever: 55–10 over the Denver Broncos.

SUPER HUMAN

If not for the 49ers, fans might have talked about the Cincinnati Bengals as one of the top teams of the 1980s. The Bengals reached the Super Bowl twice in the decade, but ran into quarterback Joe Montana and the 49ers each time. "Joe Montana is not human," Cincinnati star wide receiver Cris Collinsworth said after Super Bowl XXIII. "He's not God, either, but he's somewhere in between."

BAD TIMING

The toughest luck of the 1980s belonged to the AFC's Denver Broncos. They made it to the Super Bowl three times, but ran into a different NFC buzz saw each time: first, the New York Giants, then the Washington Redskins, and then the San Francisco 49ers. Still, the Broncos gave football fans "The Drive" in the 1986 AFC Championship Game against Cleveland. That long touchdown march is one of the most famous in NFL history. It came late in the fourth quarter and sent the game into overtime. Denver eventually won the game to make it to Super Bowl XXI.

More Champions of the 1980s

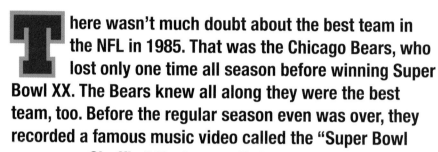

There wasn't much doubt about the best team in the NFL in 1985. That was the Chicago Bears, who lost only one time all season before winning Super Bowl XX. The Bears knew all along they were the best team, too. Before the regular season even was over, they recorded a famous music video called the "Super Bowl Shuffle." That was a little cocky, but the Bears backed it up.

Chicago played a blitzing, intimidating new defense called the "46 Defense." Opposing quarterbacks didn't have time to think about where to throw the ball. In the NFC playoffs, the Bears posted shutouts over the New York Giants and the Los Angeles Rams. In the Super Bowl, Chicago and the 46 Defense overwhelmed the New England Patriots, 46–10.

THE HOGS

"Hogs" doesn't sound like a particularly nice nickname, but the Washington Redskins loved it. That was the nickname of the team's offensive line in the 1980s. Playing offensive line is not a glamorous job, but the Redskins' "Hogs" took pride in leading the way for bruising running back John Riggins. With Riggins rushing for the go-ahead touchdown in the fourth quarter, Washington beat the Miami Dolphins 27–17 in Super Bowl XVII in the 1982 season. Five years later, the Redskins routed the Denver Broncos 42–10 in Super Bowl XXII.

JUST WIN, BABY

When the AFC and the NFC were created in 1970, the NFL began allowing one wild-card team from each conference into the playoffs. (A wild-card team is the non-division winner with the best record; since 1978, two wild-card teams from each conference have made the playoffs.) No wild-card team won the Super Bowl until the Oakland Raiders won game XV in the 1980 season.

That year, the Raiders finished second to the San Diego Chargers in the AFC's Western Division. Oakland won three playoff games, the last against the Chargers, to make it to the Super Bowl against the Philadelphia Eagles. "Just win, baby," Raiders owner Al Davis told his team. The Eagles were champions of the NFC East, but the game was no contest. Oakland won 27–10.

Super Bowl Dynasties:
THE STEEL CURTAIN

Football was a lot different in the 1970s than it is today. Back then, defense was the name of the game. Games were lower scoring. Teams ran the ball a lot on offense, and they relied on their defense to win games. No team had a better defense in the 1970s—and no team won more Super Bowls—than the Pittsburgh Steelers. Those Pittsburgh teams had one of the best defenses in NFL history, and one of the most famous nicknames: the "Steel Curtain."

"Mean Joe" Greene anchored the Steel Curtain's defensive line. Jack Ham and Jack Lambert were tackling machines at linebacker. Cornerback Mel Blount intimidated opposing pass catchers. The Steelers shut down the Minnesota Vikings to win Super Bowl IX 16–6 in the 1974 season. Then they beat the Dallas Cowboys 21–17 in Super Bowl X.

Near the end of the decade, the NFL changed some rules to help offenses score more points. Teams started passing the ball more. That included the Steelers. They won Super Bowls XIII and XIV with quarterback Terry Bradshaw putting the ball in the air a lot more. Still, it is the "Steel Curtain" for which this Super Bowl dynasty is mostly known.

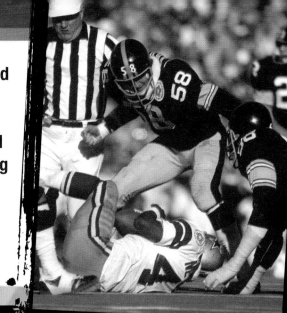

NAME GAME

The Steelers weren't the only Super Bowl team in the 1970s with a cool nickname. The Dallas Cowboys had the "Doomsday Defense." The Miami Dolphins had a great defense, but not many stars, so they had the "No-Name Defense." The Los Angeles Rams didn't make the Super Bowl until the 1979 season, but earlier in the decade, they were a contender because of their "Fearsome Foursome" defensive line.

In Minnesota, the Vikings got to the Super Bowl three times in the decade—they lost each time—on the strength of their "Purple People Eaters" defense. At least one Vikings' player, though, didn't like the nickname. Said star defensive tackle Carl Eller: "I'm not purple, and I don't eat people!"

THAT NAME IS FAMILIAR

Terry Bradshaw was a star quarterback for the Steelers from 1970 to 1983. In 1989, he was inducted into the Pro Football Hall of Fame. You might recognize Bradshaw from somewhere else, though: television! Bradshaw has been in several movies and television shows since retiring from football, and for more than 25 years has been an NFL game or studio analyst. He's currently part of Fox Television's Sunday NFL studio crew.

More Champions of the 1970s

The 1972 Miami Dolphins were the first, and still only, perfect team in NFL history. A few other NFL teams have won all their regular-season games, but then lost in the postseason (most recently, the 2007 New England Patriots). Miami, though, won all 14 of its regular-season games in 1972. Then they beat the Cleveland Browns and the Pittsburgh Steelers in close games in the playoffs. The Dolphins capped their perfect season by beating the Washington Redskins 14–7 in Super Bowl VII.

Even though Miami had won 16 times in 16 games, the Redskins were favored to win Super Bowl VII. The game was close, but Washington had trouble scoring against the Dolphins' defense.

Miami won the Super Bowl again the following season. They weren't perfect that time, but they lost only two games all year before beating the Minnesota Vikings 24–7 in Super Bowl VIII.

DOOMSDAY IN DALLAS

It wasn't quite the Steel Curtain, but the Dallas Cowboys had a pretty good defense in the 1970s, too. The "Doomsday Defense" helped the Cowboys beat the Miami Dolphins 24–3 in Super Bowl VI in the 1971 season. Six years later, "Doomsday II" helped Dallas beat Denver 27–10 in Super Bowl XII. In that game, the Cowboys' defense recovered four fumbles and intercepted four of Denver quarterback Craig Morton's passes. It was a not-so-friendly reunion for Morton. He used to play quarterback for Dallas!

NERVOUS TIME

In 1970, the first year after the NFL and the American Football League (AFL) merged to form one league, the Baltimore Colts joined the newly formed AFC. (To make it so there were an equal number of teams in both the NFC and the AFC, the NFL's Colts, Cleveland Browns, and Pittsburgh Steelers joined the 10 former AFL teams.) The Colts were the first champions of the new, and bigger, NFL. Baltimore beat the Dallas Cowboys 16–13 when Jim O'Brien kicked a field goal with five seconds left. The rookie was so nervous before his winning kick that he tried to pick up a blade of grass to gauge the wind. Only one problem: The game was played on artificial turf!

Vince Lombardi is probably the most famous football coach ever. Lombardi was a tough, disciplined, hard-working man. When he became the head coach of the Green Bay Packers, he wanted his teams to be the same way: tough, disciplined, and hard-working. The Packers followed their coach's example so well that they were the NFL's best team of the 1960s, and they won the first two Super Bowls ever played.

Before Lombardi became the coach in Green Bay in 1959, the Packers hadn't been very good for a while. They had gone 11 years in a row without a winning season. Lombardi quickly changed that. In his first year, Green Bay won 7 games and lost 5. In his second year, the Packers made it to the NFL Championship Game. In his third year, they won the league title.

There was no Super Bowl back then, though. The Super Bowl didn't start until the 1966 season. Naturally, the Packers were in it—and the game wasn't even close. Green Bay beat the Kansas City Chiefs of the AFL 35–10. The next year, Green Bay won it again, beating the Oakland Raiders 33–14.

VICTORY RIDE

Vince Lombardi hadn't officially announced that he was stepping down as coach of the Green Bay Packers after Super Bowl II, but his players had a pretty good idea it was coming. So after Lombardi's Packers blasted the Oakland Raiders 33–14 in that game, his players hoisted him on their shoulders and carried him off the field at the Orange Bowl stadium in Miami, Florida. "It's the best way to leave a football field," Lombardi said later.

A BIG DEAL

The Packers were the representatives of the NFL in the first Super Bowl. That was a big deal to them because they were playing the champions of the AFL (the Kansas City Chiefs). The two leagues were big rivals. They tried to get the same players to play for them and, in some cases, the same fans to root for them. Green Bay coach Vince Lombardi was nervous about upholding the honor of the more established NFL. He didn't have to worry so much. The Packers won the game easily.

More Champions of the 1960s

After the NFL's Green Bay Packers won the first two Super Bowls so easily, a lot of folks wondered if the AFL was good enough. In Super Bowl III in the 1968 season, the New York Jets proved the younger league sure was good enough.

Jets quarterback Joe Namath guaranteed during the week that his team would win, and then he led his team to a 16–7 victory over the Baltimore Colts. It was a huge upset. The Colts were a powerful team and were expected to win by three touchdowns or more. It was an historic win that gave the AFL credibility ahead of the impending merger between the NFL and AFL that would take full effect in the 1970 season.

Some fans still figured the Jets' win was just a fluke. But the next year, the Kansas City Chiefs won another Super Bowl for the AFL by beating the NFL's Minnesota Vikings 23–7.

SUPER NAME

Did you know that the Super Bowl wasn't called the Super Bowl at first? It was called the "AFL-NFL World Championship Game." That name doesn't have quite the same ring to it! They didn't start calling it the Super Bowl until game III in the 1968 season. Kansas City Chiefs owner Lamar Hunt got the idea for the name after watching his kids play with a Super Ball.

XLIV, NOT 44

Ever wonder why they use Roman numerals instead of ordinary numbers to keep track of which Super Bowl is which? While it's true that Roman numerals give the game a sense of importance, that's not why. The real reason is because the NFL regular season and the Super Bowl are played in different calendar years. (For instance, the Super Bowl for the 2009 season was played in February of 2010.) With Roman numerals, there's no confusing the season and the Super Bowl.

SUPER-LATIVES!

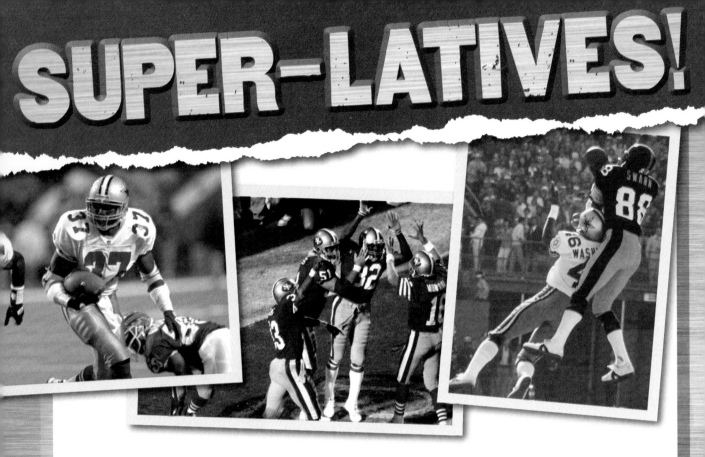

What team has played in the Super Bowl the most times? The Dallas Cowboys. (Maybe that's why they're called "America's Team.") Dallas has played in the Super Bowl eight times, winning five. The San Francisco 49ers also have won five Super Bowls, and have never lost in the Big Game. The Pittsburgh Steelers are the only team to win the Super Bowl six times, though. They have played in a total of seven Super Bowls.

THERE'S A FIRST TIME FOR EVERYONE

With the New Orleans Saints making it to game XLIV, almost every team has been to the Super Bowl at least once. The only teams still looking for their first trip to the Big Game are the Cleveland Browns, Detroit Lions, Jacksonville Jaguars (who only began play in 1995), and the Houston Texans (who started in 2002).

50 PLUS

The most number of points any team has scored in the Super Bowl is 55. The San Francisco 49ers beat the Denver Broncos 55–10 in Super Bowl XXIV. The Dallas Cowboys came close to that total when they beat the Buffalo Bills 52–17 in Super Bowl XXVII.

TOP FIVE

Everybody has their own opinion about the best Super Bowls ever. In no particular order, here are five of the best:

- **Pittsburgh 27, Arizona 23** (Super Bowl XLIII)
- **N.Y. Giants 20, Buffalo 19** (Super Bowl XXV)
- **San Francisco 20, Cincinnati 16** (Super Bowl XXIII)
- **Pittsburgh 35, Dallas 31** (Super Bowl XIII)
- **N.Y. Giants 17, New England 14** (Super Bowl XLII)

ALL FOUR WON

Only two quarterbacks have led their teams to four Super Bowl wins: the Pittsburgh Steelers' Terry Bradshaw and the San Francisco 49ers' Joe Montana. Only one coach has won the Super Bowl four times. That was the Steelers' Chuck Noll. None of those men ever wound up on the losing side in a Super Bowl.

TO THE VICTORS GO THE SPOILS

The ultimate symbol of NFL achievement is the Vince Lombardi Trophy. It's the trophy presented to the winning team in the Super Bowl each season.

The trophy is made each year in New Jersey by Tiffany and Co., the famous jewelry and silverware company. It takes four months to make the trophy, which is a regulation-sized football atop a base. It's 21 inches high, weighs 7 pounds, and is made entirely by hand from sterling silver.

The trophy originally was called the AFL-NFL World Championship Trophy, but was renamed in honor of the legendary Vince Lombardi in 1970. Each Lombardi Trophy is valued at about $25,000. But to the winning team owner who hoists the trophy on the presentation stand after the Super Bowl, it's priceless.

VINCE LOMBARDI
TROPHY

NFL

PETE ROZELLE TROPHY

The Most Valuable Player in the Super Bowl is awarded the Pete Rozelle Trophy. It's named after the NFL commissioner who helped the Super Bowl grow so much. (Rozelle was commissioner from 1960 to 1989.)

The Pete Rozelle Trophy almost always goes to a player from the winning team. In fact, a player from the losing team has been named the MVP only once. That was in Super Bowl V, when Dallas Cowboys linebacker Chuck Howley earned the award even though his team lost a close game to the Baltimore Colts.

THE RING'S THE THING

Ask almost any NFL player, and he'll tell you he doesn't play for the glory or the money, he plays for the ring. "The ring" is a Super Bowl ring, which is earned by members of the winning team in the Big Game.

Super Bowl rings aren't the kinds of rings you casually wear out in public. The Packers' original rings for winning Super Bowl I look somewhat like a normal college class ring (only for football-player-sized fingers!). But rings have grown along with the game over the years. The Steelers' 14-karat-gold rings for winning Super Bowl XLIII in the 2008 season weighed about 3.7 ounces and incorporated 63 round, brilliant-cut diamonds totaling 3.61 carats. The diamonds included six larger, round diamonds to signify the franchise's six all-time Super Bowl wins. The rings, which are made by Jostens, Inc., usually cost about $5,000 to make.

The Record Book

All-Time Super Bowl Results

GAME	SEASON	SCORE
I	1966	Green Bay 35, Kansas City 10
II	1967	Green Bay 33, Oakland 14
III	1968	N.Y. Jets 16, Baltimore 7
IV	1969	Kansas City 23, Minnesota 7
V	1970	Baltimore 16, Dallas 13
VI	1971	Dallas 24, Miami 3
VII	1972	Miami 14, Washington 7
VIII	1973	Miami 24, Minnesota 7
IX	1974	Pittsburgh 16, Minnesota 6
X	1975	Pittsburgh 21, Dallas 17
XI	1976	Oakland 32, Minnesota 14
XII	1977	Dallas 27, Denver 10
XIII	1978	Pittsburgh 35, Dallas 31
XIV	1979	Pittsburgh 31, Los Angeles 19
XV	1980	Oakland 27, Philadelphia 10
XVI	1981	San Francisco 26, Cincinnati 21
XVII	1982	Washington 27, Miami 17
XVIII	1983	L.A. Raiders 38, Washington 9
XIX	1984	San Francisco 38, Miami 16
XX	1985	Chicago 46, New England 10
XXI	1986	N.Y. Giants 39, Denver 20
XXII	1987	Washington 42, Denver 10
XXIII	1988	San Francisco 20, Cincinnati 16
XXIV	1989	San Francisco 55, Denver 10
XXV	1990	N.Y. Giants 20, Buffalo 19
XXVI	1991	Washington 37, Buffalo 24
XXVII	1992	Dallas 52, Buffalo 17
XXVIII	1993	Dallas 30, Buffalo 13
XXIX	1994	San Francisco 49, San Diego 26
XXX	1995	Dallas 27, Pittsburgh 17
XXXI	1996	Green Bay 35, New England 21
XXXII	1997	Denver 31, Green Bay 24
XXXIII	1998	Denver 34, Atlanta 19
XXXIV	1999	St. Louis 23, Tennessee 16
XXXV	2000	Baltimore 34, N.Y. Giants 7
XXXVI	2001	New England 20, St. Louis 17
XXXVII	2002	Tampa Bay 48, Oakland 21
XXXVIII	2003	New England 32, Carolina 29
XXXIX	2004	New England 24, Philadelphia 21
XL	2005	Pittsburgh 21, Seattle 10
XLI	2006	Indianapolis 29, Chicago 17
XLII	2007	N.Y. Giants 17, New England 14
XLIII	2008	Pittsburgh 27, Arizona 23
XLIV	2009	New Orleans 31, Indianapolis 17

All-Time Super Bowl Standings

	W	L
San Francisco 49ers	5	0
Baltimore Ravens	1	0
New Orleans Saints	1	0
New York Jets	1	0
Tampa Bay Buccaneers	1	0
Pittsburgh Steelers	6	1
Green Bay Packers	3	1
New York Giants	3	1
Dallas Cowboys	5	3
Oakland/L.A. Raiders	3	2
Washington Redskins	3	2
New England Patriots	3	3
Indianapolis/Baltimore Colts	2	2
Chicago Bears	1	1
Kansas City Chiefs	1	1
Miami Dolphins	2	3
Denver Broncos	2	4
St. Louis/L.A. Rams	1	2
Arizona Cardinals	0	1
Atlanta Falcons	0	1
Carolina Panthers	0	1
San Diego Chargers	0	1
Seattle Seahawks	0	1
Tennessee Titans	0	1
Cincinnati Bengals	0	2
Philadelphia Eagles	0	2
Buffalo Bills	0	4
Minnesota Vikings	0	4

A list of pieces making use of FINGER STACCATO will be found on page 44.

Forearm Staccato

In this touch the elbow is the hinge.

When in mid-air the hand hangs loosely from the wrist. At the moment of impact with the keys, the wrist drops to normal (level) position.

This touch makes more use of the Weight Principle than wrist staccato and the result is a staccato with more depth of tone.

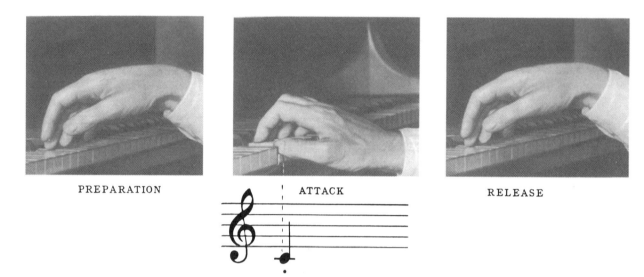

PREPARATION   ATTACK   RELEASE

The Freight Train

See page 44 for list of pieces requiring FOREARM STACCATO.

W. M Co. 5763

Portamento

Portamento in piano music, means a long (sustained) note, detached from the following note and is indicated by the curved line and the dots thus.

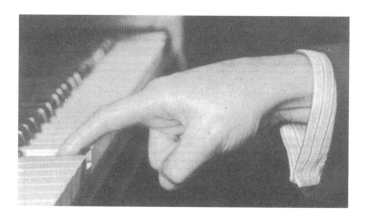

It is produced by the forearm in a slightly forward motion. Use practically the same motion as for Forearm staccato, only give to each note more resonance and longer duration.

The best way to get the "feel" of this stroke is to play the C major scale as legato as possible *with one finger*, held as shown in the accompanying picture.

The Steamboat

on

W. M. Co. 5763

Close Finger Legato
Quiet Hand

For this touch, keep the **fingers** close to the keys, allowing the weight of the hand to be transferred from one finger to the other.
DONT PUSH. Both hand and arm remain *perfectly quiet*. Think of *walking on the fingers*.

This touch develops *evenness* of tone – since the arm weighs the same on each finger. It produces a "liquid" quality in passage work and makes possible more speed – as less finger effort is expended.

Aquaplaning

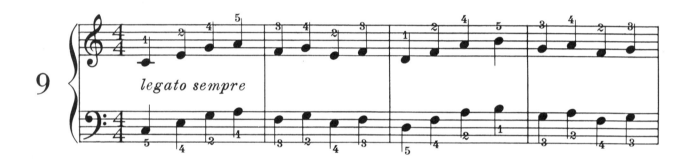

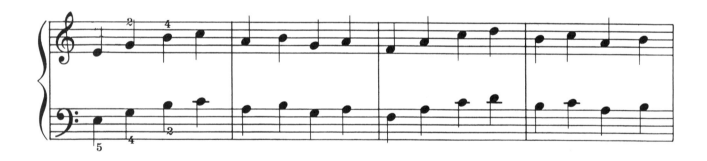

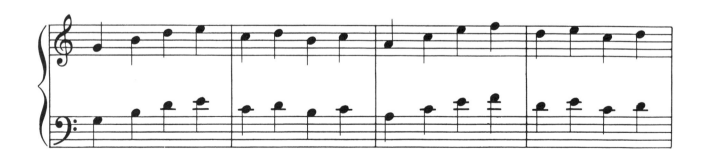

See page 44 for list of pieces containing CLOSE FINGER LEGATO.

W. M. Co. 5763

Rotary Motion
Rolling Attack

In this touch, no finger action whatever is used.
Think of the hand as a wheel, the fingers of which are the spokes.
When the hand (or wheel) is rolled in either direction, the fingers (**spokes**) play as they come in contact with the keys.
Be sure to toss off the last note of the roll sharply, using the same inward and upward motion as that applied to the last note (rolled) when finishing a phrase.

This touch gives to a passage almost the effect of a glissando.

The Fountain

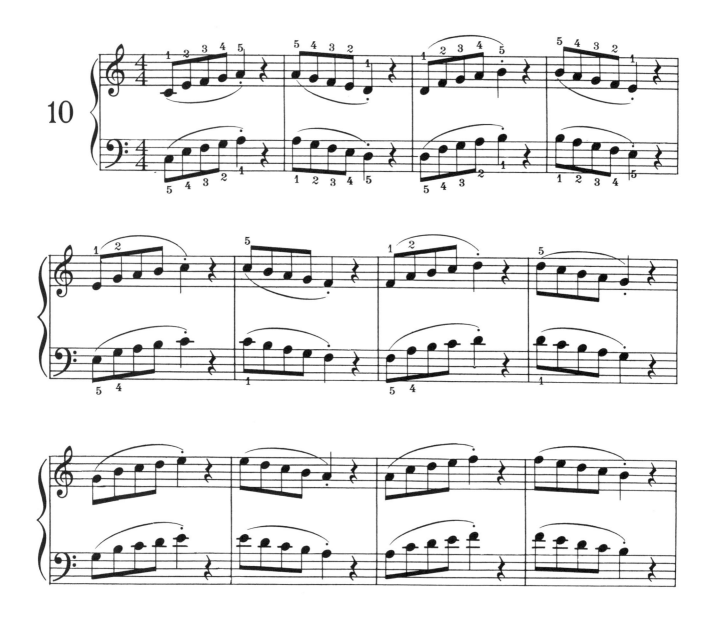

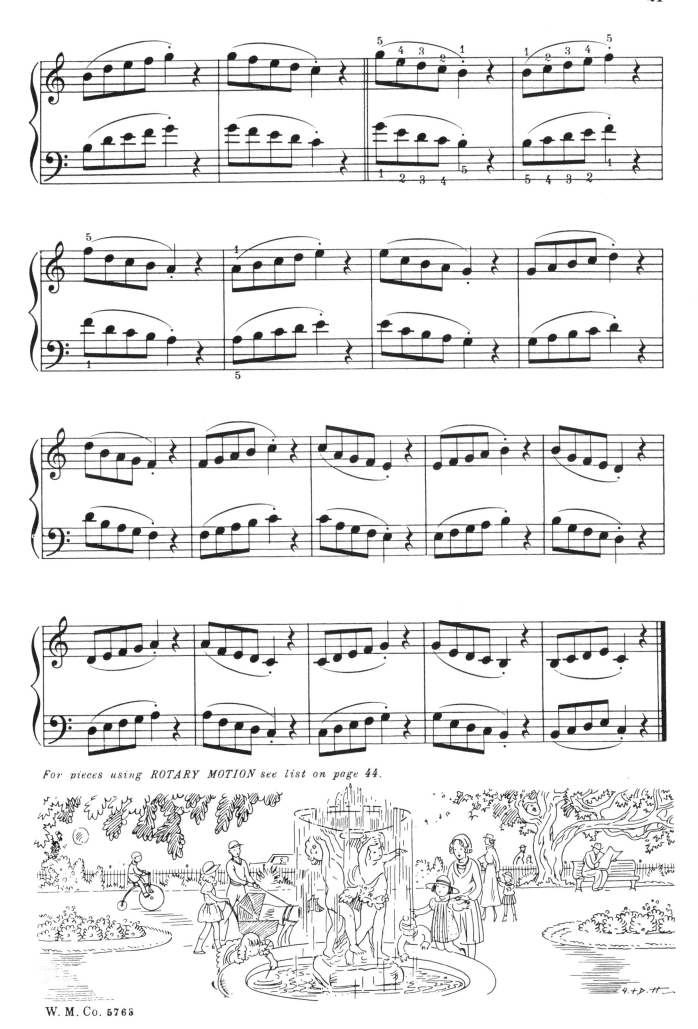

For pieces using *ROTARY MOTION* see list on page **44**.

W. M. Co. 5763

NOTE

At this point, review the first ten studies, playing each one in all of the various rhythms shown in the following examples.

This procedure obviates monotonous repetition and results in added interest, enforced concentration and, not of least importance, *speed* will develop automatically if the rhythms are followed in the order given.

When the first Ten Exercises *can be played in 16ths.*, proceed to Section Two, page 24.

During the review work of Section One, various attacks may be employed at the discretion of the teacher.

However, it is well to *stress* the use of *High* and *Close Finger Legato* in all the studies since, after all, the *primary purpose* of the Hanon Studies is to develop strong and agile finger action.

It is important that the pupil strive to play these studies with Tonal Gradation. Crescendo and Diminuendo may be applied at will, according to the taste of the pupil or, as directed by the teacher.

Rhythmical Drills
for
Developing Speed
Motif from Exercise No. I

Alternating Long and Short Phrases

Yachting

11

A list of pieces containing LONG AND SHORT PHRASES will be found on page 44.

W. M. Co. 5763

Alternating Short and Long Phrases

The Glider

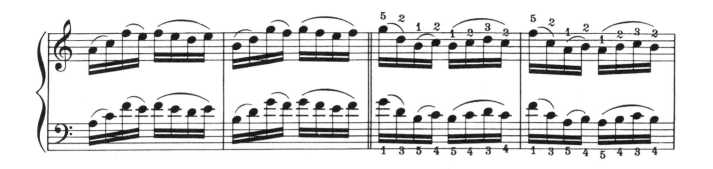

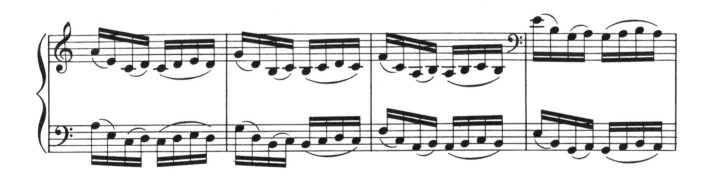

See page 44 for list of pieces containing SHORT AND LONG PHRASES.

W. M. Co. 5763

Alternating Legato and Wrist Staccato

The Bee and the Cricket

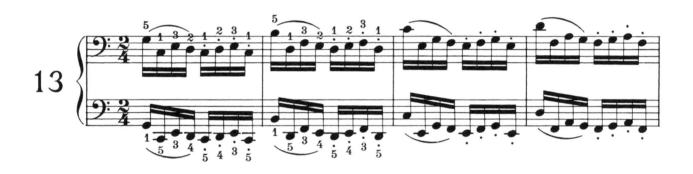

*See page **44** for list of pieces requiring both LEGATO and STACCATO touches.*

W. M. Co. 5763

Alternating Staccato and Legato

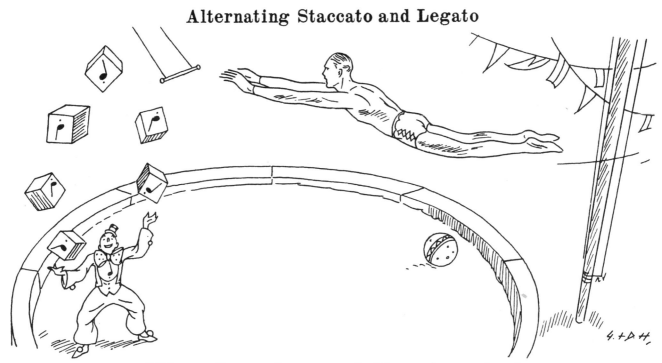

The Juggler and the Acrobat

W. M. Co. 5768

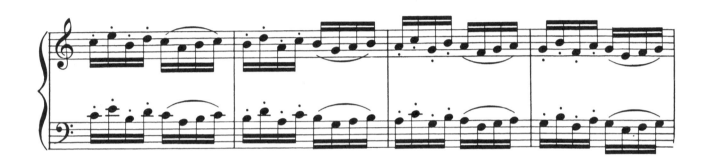

See page 44 for list of pieces requiring both STACCATO and LEGATO touch.

W. M. Co. 5763

Combining the Various Touches

At the Fair

Slurred Groups (Expanding)

Balloon Race
The Take-off

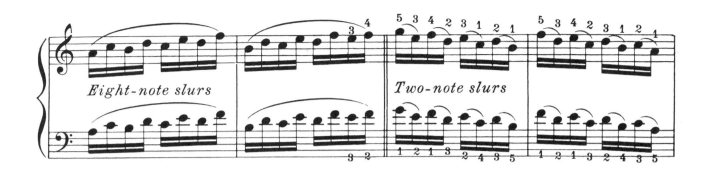

Slurred Groups (Contracting)

Balloon Race
The Landing

W. M. Co. 5768

Combined Touches as directed by the Teacher

In this Exercise the teacher should call for a different touch every two measures. The pupil must be prepared to change from one touch to the other without hesitation.

18
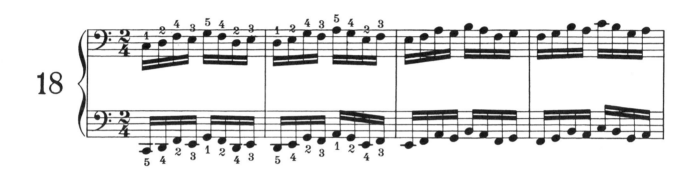

W. M. Co. 5763

Interlocking Staccato and Legato

This Exercise should be studied until the pupil can change from staccato to legato without effort.

Various staccato touches may be used at the direction of the teacher.

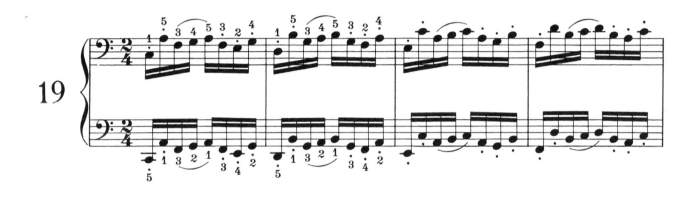

W. M. Co. 5763

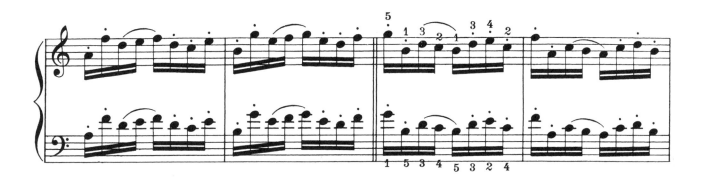

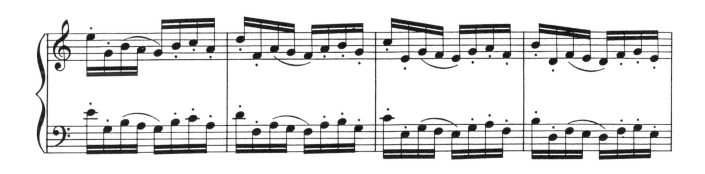

See page 44 for list of pieces combining LEGATO and STACCATO touches.

W. M. Co. 5763

42

Combining Rotary Motion with Close Finger Legato

Practice this Exercise first using High Finger Legato throughout.

Later roll the arpeggio groups (first half of each measure) and use Close Finger Legato

on the last half of each measure, thus:

The Swallow

W. M. Co. **5763** When the student has finished this book we strongly recommend that he proceed immediately to JOHN THOMPSON'S HANON — BOOK TWO, especially edited by John Thompson — WMCo., edition 9345.

RECOMMENDED TEACHING PIECES

Classified according to Touch

TWO-NOTE PHRASES

SWAYING SILVER BIRCHES....Leslie—Gr. 1
DUTCH TWINS..............Ward—Gr. 1
FOREST DAWN.........Thompson—Gr. 1
HIAWATHA'S LULLABY.......Ward—Gr. 2
ON A SUMMER SEA.......Ketterer—Gr. 2
BROWNIES' CARNIVAL....Thompson—Gr. 2
ROGUISH EYES............Haines—Gr. 2
TANGO CARIOCA.......Thompson—Gr. 3

THREE-NOTE PHRASES

COBBLER, COBBLER.........Rebe—Gr. 1
MOCCASIN DANCE...........Long—Gr. 1
CAPTAIN KIDD.............Waldo—Gr. 2
MARCH OF THE CHAMPIONS..Waldo—Gr. 3

ALTERNATING LONG AND SHORT PHRASES

DROWSY MOON..............Long—Gr. 2
ROGUISH EYES............Haines—Gr. 2

HIGH FINGER LEGATO

LULLABY.......Brahms-Thompson—Gr. 1
MARCHE SLAV
          Tchaikowsky-Thompson—Gr. 1

CLOSE FINGER LEGATO

BUSY CORNERS........Montandon—Gr. 2
WOODS AT DAWN...........Kerr—Gr. 2

FINGER STACCATO

MARCH OF THE SPOOKS......Haines—Gr. 1
KATYDID AND THE CRICKET..Wade—Gr. 3

WRIST STACCATO

DUTCH TWINS..............Ward—Gr. 1
MARCH OF THE SPOOKS....Haines—Gr. 1

Wrist Staccato—*Cont.*

PROCESSION OF THE SEVEN DWARFS
                        Long—Gr. 1
VALSE TRISTE...Sibelius-Thompson—Gr. 1
CHEER LEADER..........Rodgers—Gr. 2
PARADE OF THE PENGUINS....Wade—Gr. 2
DRUM MAJOR..............Selby—Gr. 3

FOREARM STACCATO

ON THE LEVEE............Waldo—Gr. 1
HOE CAKE SHUFFLE........Leslie—Gr. 1
MARCHE SLAV
          Tschaikowsky-Thompson—Gr. 1
MOCCASIN DANCE...........Long—Gr. 1
MARCH OF THE CHAMPIONS..Waldo—Gr. 3
BY A ROADSIDE FIRE......Rodgers—Gr. 3

LEGATO AND STACCATO

BOGEY MAN...............Long—Gr. 1
COBBLER, COBBLER.........Rebe—Gr. 1
HOE CAKE SHUFFLE........Leslie—Gr. 1
BROWNIES' CARNIVAL....Thompson—Gr. 2
BUSY CORNERS.......Montandon—Gr. 2
CAPTAIN KIDD............Waldo—Gr. 2
ROGUISH EYES............Haines—Gr. 2
WOODS AT DAWN...........Kerr—Gr. 2
TANGO CARIOCA.......Thompson—Gr. 3

WRIST AND ARM STACCATO

BANJO PICKER............Wright—Gr. 2
PARADE OF THE PENGUINS..Waldo—Gr. 2

ROTARY MOTION

DIRIGIBLE.............Thompson—Gr. 2
SWAN ON THE MOONLIT LAKE..Rebe—Gr. 2
BALLOONS................Arlen—Gr. 3

All of the above pieces are contained in
"JOHN THOMPSON'S STUDENTS SERIES"

THE PROGRESSIVE SUCCESSION
of
JOHN THOMPSON'S MODERN COURSE FOR THE PIANO

"SOMETHING NEW EVERY LESSON"

PREPARATORY GRADE

"Teaching Little Fingers to Play" — *A book for the earliest beginner combining ROTE and NOTE approach.*

Accompaniment Book "Teaching Little Fingers to Play Ensemble" — *With these accompaniments, teacher, parent, or advanced pupil may play each piece as a duet. The second piano part is invaluable for 2 pianos, 4 hand playing in class or recital work.*

GRADE ONE

"John Thompson's First Grade Book" — *A correct foundation for teaching the pupil to think and feel musically.*

"Hanon Studies" (*Specially edited by John Thompson*) — *Pages 2-23 (in quarter-notes) to be used for supplementary work.*

Supplementary material for diversion

"For Girls Who Play" ♪ "Covered Wagon Suite"
"Let's Join the Army" ♪ "Students Series"—*Grade 1 Teaching Pieces*

GRADE TWO

"John Thompson's Second Grade Book" — *Carries on the principles of the course "make haste slowly but learn thoroughly."*

"Hanon Studies" (*Specially edited by John Thompson*) — *Pages 24-43 to be used supplementary.*

"First Studies in Style"

Supplementary material for diversion

"The Pilgrim Suite" ♪ "Students Series"—*Grade 2 Teaching Pieces*

GRADE THREE

"John Thompson's Third Grade Book" — *Progresses uninterruptedly and logically.*

"Third Grade Velocity Studies" — (*Specially Edited by John Thompson*)

"Hanon Studies" --- Book Two — (*Specially edited by John Thompson*)

"Keyboard Attacks" ♪ "World Known Melodies"
"We're in the Navy Now" ♪ "Students Series"—*Grade 3 Teaching Pieces*

FOR SALE BY ALL MUSIC DEALERS